LATVIA

WITHDRAWN

RUSSIA

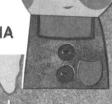

GERMANY

POLAND

INDIA

PHILIPPINES

First published in the United Kingdom in 2020 by
Lantana Publishing Ltd., London.
www.lantanapublishing.com

American edition published in 2020 by
Lantana Publishing Ltd., UK.
info@lantanapublishing.com

Distributed in the United States and Canada by
Lerner Publishing Group, Inc.
241 First Avenue North, Minneapolis, MN 55401 U.S.A.
For reading levels and more information,
look for this title at www.lernerbooks.com
Cataloging-in-Publication Data Available.

Printed and bound in China.
Original artwork using hand-printed textures
and pencils, finished digitally.

ISBN: 978-1-911373-49-0
eBook ISBN: 978-1-911373-59-9

To the hundreds of young
children with whom I've
shared many memorable
stories, and most especially,
to Marybeth.
Susan

To Manu, for all the
adventures, cultures and
languages we still have
to discover.
Raquel

"Do you see
the dragon?"

I'LL BELIEVE YOU WHEN...

LANTANA
PUBLISHING

"Dragon?
What dragon?
I'll believe you..."

...when pigs fly!

SPAIN

...when frogs grow **hair!**

...when chickens have **teeth!**

...when fish climb poplars!

...when the heron turns black!

...when cows
dance on ice!

...when crows fly
upside down!

...when the lobster whistles
on top of the mountain!

RUSSIA

...when my hand grows a **cactus!**

"Oh, THAT dragon!
Now we believe you."

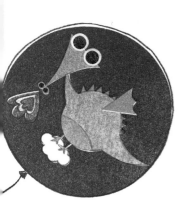

An idiom is a playful phrase that paints a wonderful "picture joke" in your mind. Imagine cows dancing on ice or frogs growing hair! What fun!

Idioms include words that often have no clear connection to each other in meaning. What do pigs have to do with flying or mountains with lobsters? On the face of it, idioms usually make little sense! Instead, their meanings come from the speaking patterns of the time or culture that coined them. They are so useful that others soon adopt them too.

What idioms do you know? Can you make up some of your own? For example, instead of "when pigs fly," you might draw snakes wearing skates or cows laying eggs!

Susan

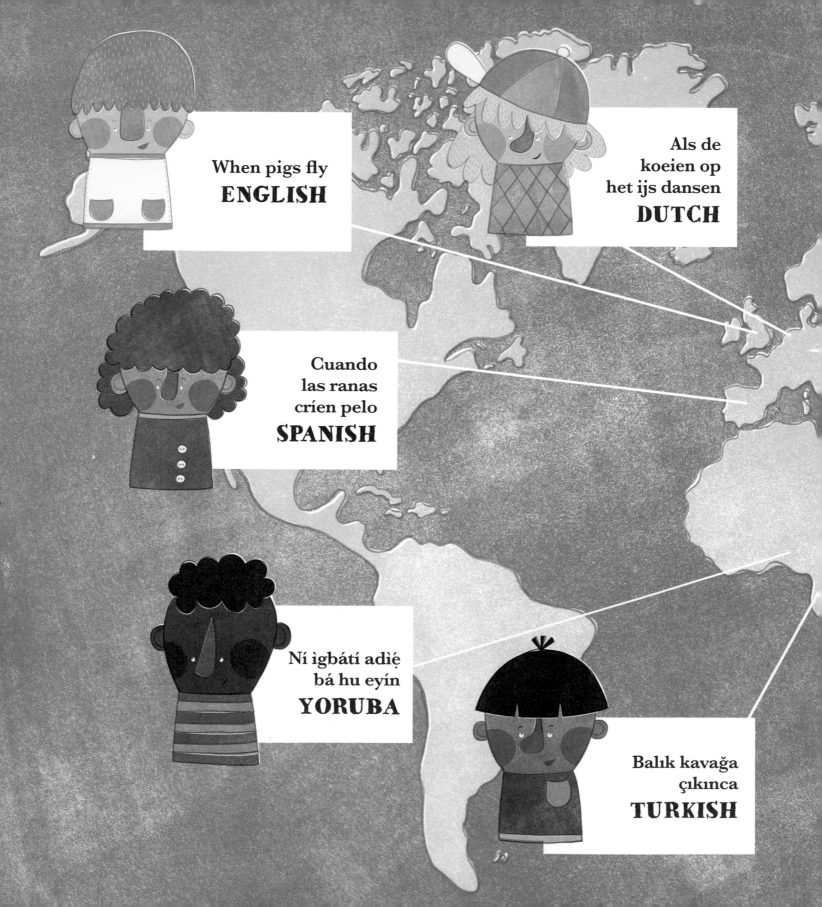